William and the Pied Piper

'This evening,' said Mrs Patel, 'we are going to put
 on our play again. Hamid is better, and we know
 our parts. This time nothing should go wrong.'
The play was called *The Pied Piper of Hamelin*.
'Why was he called the Pied Piper?' asked William.
 'Did he come out of a pie like those blackbirds?'

'No, William, no,' said Mrs Patel. 'Pied means
    brightly coloured. The Pied Piper's clothes
    were made out of patches of red and gold material.'
'Is it a true story?' asked Hamid.
'Of course it's not!' laughed William. 'It's just a fairy
    story for little children.'

2

'Don't be too sure, William,' said Mrs Patel. 'Most
   of these old stories have some truth in them. This
   story is so old that nobody knows how it started.'
'Well I don't believe it,' said William. 'I don't
   believe in giants and fairies and wolves that
   eat grandmothers.'

That evening the play was a great success.

Hamid remembered all his lines.

At the end of the play the audience clapped and
  cheered.

Mrs Patel was very pleased and excited.

'You were brilliant, Hamid,' said William. 'I know
    it's only a play but I could almost believe it
    was real.'
'It's a pity your tail came off,' said Hamid.
'Yes I know,' said William. 'Jane trod on it
    but it made everyone laugh.'

William and Hamid had to wait on the stage for
    William's mum to take them home.
'Look!' said William. 'There's a trap door in the
    stage. I wonder what it's used for?'
'Let's have a look,' said Hamid.
They opened the trap door and went down the steps.

It was very dark under the stage.

Hamid tripped over something and twisted his ankle.

'Oww!' he cried. 'I think it might be broken.
   I wish we had a torch.'

'Don't worry,' said William. 'Hold on, and I'll help
   you. Mum will be here in a minute.'

Hamid hadn't broken his ankle but it was swollen
and very sore.
The boys struggled up the steps back on to the stage.
'Something funny has happened,' gasped William.
'This isn't the school hall. Where are we?'

The boys seemed to be in an old house or shop.
It was very dirty and full of barrels and
    carpenter's tools.
'I've got a funny feeling about this,' whispered
    William. 'It looks like a picture in a book.'

'I've got a funny feeling, too,' whispered Hamid.
  'I think something is watching us. It's creepy!'
There were little scuffling and rustling sounds
  coming from all the corners of the shop.
'Rats!' gasped William. 'Quick! Let's get out of
  here. There's a door.'

William helped Hamid into the street.
Everything seemed old-fashioned and strange.
'I know where we are,' gasped Hamid. 'We're in the
    story. This must be Hamelin. Look at the clothes
    they're wearing, and all the old buildings.'

'There are rats everywhere,' said William.
'How are we going to get home?' asked Hamid.
'Everybody seems to be going into that building
   over there,' said William. 'Let's go and see if
   we can find someone to ask.'

'You'll have to help me,' said Hamid. 'I can
   hardly walk.'
The boys followed the crowds into the building.
'It must be the Town Hall,' said Hamid. 'And I
   think I know what's going to happen.'

At the front of the hall, around a big table,
    sat a lot of important looking people.
They were talking to a man dressed in brightly
    coloured clothes.
'I knew it!' whispered Hamid. 'It's the Pied Piper.'
On the table was a big bag of gold.

'They're going to offer him the gold, and he's going
    to play his pipe,' said Hamid. 'Then all the rats
    will follow him to the river and be drowned.'
At that moment the Pied Piper stood up, shook hands
    with the Lord Mayor and walked out of the hall.
But the Lord Mayor held on to the bag of gold.

Everybody followed the Pied Piper out into the
    town square.
He raised his magic pipe to his lips and began
    to play a strange but beautiful tune.
Rats ran out of all the houses and shops to listen
    to the music.

Then the Piper walked out of the town towards the
    river nearby.
When he reached the river bank he stopped.
But the rats didn't stop.
They jumped into the river and were washed away.
All the townspeople laughed and cheered.

William looked worried.

'They wouldn't be laughing and cheering like that if
   they knew what was going to happen next,' he said.

Everybody followed the Lord Mayor and the Pied
   Piper back to the Town Hall.

'They won't pay him the money,' said Hamid.

The Lord Mayor put the bag of gold on the table.
He took out one coin and offered it to the Piper.
The Piper looked very angry.
'If they don't pay him,' whispered William, 'he will
    play his pipe again and lead all the children to
    the cave in the mountains. We've got to save them.'

The Piper walked angrily from the hall.

'I'm going to see he gets the money,' said William.

'I don't see how you can,' said Hamid. 'We'll have
    to get away or we'll end up in the cave too.'

The boys were standing near the big table.

William grabbed the gold and dashed into the street.

'Wait for me, William,' called Hamid. 'My ankle
    hurts! I can't run!'
All the townspeople began to shout.
They ran after William but they couldn't catch him.
William darted in and out of the narrow streets.
He had no idea where he was going.

In the town the Piper was playing his pipe again.
All the children had come out to listen to him.
Then he began to play a strange but beautiful tune.
He walked slowly along the road that led to the
    mountains, and the children followed him.

William was hiding among the trees along the
mountain road.
He watched the Piper lead the children past his
hiding place.
Hamid was at the back of the group of children.
He was finding it difficult to keep up.

When the children had gone past, William ran
  to Hamid.
'My ankle hurts,' said Hamid. 'I want to stop but
  I can't. It must be a magic tune.'
'It is a magic tune,' gasped William. 'I can hear it.
  I must follow it too.'
'We mustn't!' said Hamid. 'We'll be shut in the cave.'

'If only I could get to the Piper, I could give him
  this gold,' said William. 'Then perhaps he'd
  let the children go home.'
'But you know he won't,' said Hamid. 'It's not
  what happens in the story.'
'I've got to try!' said William.

By now Hamid was a long way behind all
   the other children.
William had made his way to the front of the group.
The children had reached a steep rock face on the
   side of the mountain.

A huge door was opening slowly.

'William! Don't go in,' shouted Hamid.

He could see William trying to talk to the Piper.

The Piper continued to play his pipe.

He took no notice of what William was saying.

The Piper, William, and all the children, except
   Hamid, went through the door in the mountain.
It closed slowly behind them.
William threw down the gold at the Piper's feet.
'There's your money!' he cried. 'Please let us go.'

'I hate this story,' said William. 'It's not the
children's fault that the Lord Mayor cheated you.
You can't keep them locked in here forever. There's
got to be a happy ending.'
The Piper looked at William and smiled.
'I don't like the ending, either,' he said.

Slowly, the door in the mountain opened again.
The children walked out into the sunlight.
'William!' shouted Hamid. 'I thought you were
   trapped in there forever.'
'So did I,' smiled William. 'But we still don't
   know how we're going to get home.'

Back in the town everybody was looking for William
   and the gold he had taken.
'There he is!' shouted the Lord Mayor. 'Where's
   our gold? You won't escape this time!'
'Here's the carpenter's shop,' said Hamid. 'We'd
   better hide in here. Be quick, William!'

The boys managed to get into the cellar of the shop
  and close the trap door behind them.
'They're sure to find us,' whispered Hamid.
The trap door swung open.
'Why are you down there?' said William's mum.
  'I've been waiting here for you for ages.'